# GITA FOR YUVA

## Wisdom of a Dynamic Man

Compiled by Swami Mitrananda and Yuvaveers

CENTRAL CHINMAYA MISSION TRUST

First Edition Printed by Chinmaya Udghosh Publications
First Printed - August 2010 to June 2012- 4,500 copies
Second Edition - September 2013 to August 2024 - 21,100 copies
Reprint - August 2025 - 4,000 copies

Published by:
**Chinmaya Prakashan**
The Publications Division of
**Central Chinmaya Mission Trust**
Sandeepany Sadhanalaya
Saki Vihar Road, Powai, Mumbai 400072, India
Tel.: +91-22-2803 4900
Email: ccmtpublications@chinmayamission.com
Website: www.chinmayamission.com

Distribution Centre in the USA:
**Chinmaya Mission West**
Publications Division
560 Bridgetown Pike
Feasterville, PA 19053-7240, USA
Tel.: (215) 396-0390, Fax: (215) 396-9710
Email: publications@chinmayamission.org
Website: www.chinmayapublications.com

Designed by: Chinmaya Udghosh

Printed by: SAP Print Solutions Pvt. Ltd., Mumbai

ISBN 978-81-7597-595-8

# धर्मक्षेत्रे कुरुक्षेत्रे...

## Dharmakṣetre Kurukṣetre...

Have you ever thought that the *Bhagvad-gītā* is only for the old, wrinkled and retired? Well, if you have, you could not be more wrong. The witty wisdom of this timeless book can enlighten anyone of any age, in any corner of the world.

If you are as curious and capable as the best archer of his time, young Arjuna, then this book is for you too. The intelligent advice Lord Kṛṣṇa deals out to his dear friend Arjuna is powerful, practical and potentially life-changing.

The *Gītā*, written in the form of a hearty dialogue between these two dynamic characters, is worth our while today. It is an unmatched antidote to the problems young people face, all around the globe from every walk of life. The *Gītā* creates in its readers a universal outlook and a new zeal for life.

This book presents a select 70 verses from the voluminous chapters of the *Gītā* – delicious chunks of knowledge no youngster should miss. So flip the page to read a bit of ancient wisdom repackaged for the modern mindset.

New perspectives and refreshing ideas are guaranteed. Who knows? Your life might change.

भीष्मद्रोणप्रमुखतः सर्वेषां च महीक्षिताम् ।
उवाच पार्थ पश्यैतान् समवेतान्कुरूनिति ।।१-२५।।

*bhīṣmadroṇapramukhataḥ sarveṣāṁ ca mahīkṣitām,*
*uvāca pārtha paśyaitān samavetānkurūniti.* (1-25)

In front of the great teachers and the rulers of the earth, Kṛṣṇa said, "O Bhāratīya, look at your opponents gathered together."

**Watch**

O Son of this Great Land!
Assess your mighty opponents and
face them in the Game of Life.

क्लैब्यं मा स्म गमः पार्थ नैतत्त्वय्युपपद्यते ।
क्षुद्रं हृदयदौर्बल्यं त्यक्त्वोत्तिष्ठ परंतप ।।२-३।।

*klaibyaṁ mā sma gamaḥ pārtha naitattvayyupapadyate,*
*kṣudraṁ hṛdayadaurbalyaṁ tyaktvottiṣṭha parantapa. (2-3)*

Do not give in to impotence, O Arjuna! It does not suit you. Cast off this terrible weakness of heart! Stand up, destroy your enemies.

## Get Up

Shed your incompetency.
Defeat the defeatist in you.
Get up. Get ready.
Face the challenge.

मात्रास्पर्शास्तु कौन्तेय शीतोष्णसुखदुःखदाः ।
आगमापायिनोऽनित्यास्तांस्तितिक्षस्व भारत ।।२-१४।।

*mātrāsparśāstu kaunteya śītoṣṇasukhaduḥkhadāḥ,*
*āgamāpāyino'nityāstāṁstitikṣasva bhārata. (2-14)*

When a mind makes contact with the world, you will experience heat and cold, pain and pleasure. Remember, O Arjuna, they all have a beginning and an end. None of these will stay forever, therefore endure them courageously.

## Stay Steady

All experiences, whether you like them or not, are merely temporary. So face them bravely with the constant awareness that
"Even this will pass away".

वासांसि जीर्णानि यथा विहाय नवानि गृह्णाति नरोऽपराणि ।
तथा शरीराणि विहाय जीर्णान्यन्यानि संयाति नवानि देही ।।२-२२।।

*vāsāṁsi jīrṇāni yathā vihāya navāni gṛhṇāti naro'parāṇi,*
*tathā śarīrāṇi vihāya jīrṇānyanyāni saṁyāti navāni dehī.* (2-22)

The bodies are for the indweller just like garments are for the body. Just as we discard worn garments, the indweller discards worn out bodies and accepts new ones.

## Your Death is Dead

Death is just the soul's transition from one body to the next.
Bodies are mere garments for the soul, which is deathless.

जातस्य हि ध्रुवो मृत्युर्ध्रुवं जन्म मृतस्य च ।
तस्मादपरिहार्येऽर्थे न त्वं शोचितुमर्हसि ।।२-२७।।

*jātasya hi dhruvo mṛtyurdhruvaṁ janma mṛtasya ca,*
*tasmādaparihārye'rthe na tvaṁ śocitumarhasi. (2-27)*

In fact, death is certain for the born, and birth is certain for the dead. Therefore, you should not grieve over the inevitable.

## Here I Come!

Birth and death are unavoidable facts of life.
Face it with the attitude, "Here I come!"

कर्मण्येवाधिकारस्ते मा फलेषु कदाचन ।
मा कर्मफलहेतुर्भूर्मा ते सङ्गोऽस्त्वकर्मणि ।।२-४७।।

*karmaṇyevādhikāraste mā phaleṣu kadācana,*
*mā karmaphalaheturbhūrmā te saṅgo'stvakarmaṇi.* (2-47)

Do not let the result of work distract you while performing your work. May you never give in to inaction.

## The Gift of NOW

Bring your best to each moment.
Work joyfully HERE and NOW.
Do not let your thoughts about the future distract
or discourage you from your work.

योगस्थः कुरु कर्माणि सङ्गं त्यक्त्वा धनञ्जय ।
सिद्ध्यसिद्ध्योः समो भूत्वा समत्वं योग उच्यते ।।२-४८।।

*yogasthaḥ kuru karmāṇi saṅgaṁ tyaktvā dhanañjaya,*
*siddhyasiddhyoḥ samo bhūtvā samatvaṁ yoga ucyate.* (2-48)

Devoid of attachment to success and failure, execute your responsibilities with an even mind, O, Winner of wealth. Balance of mind is Yoga.

## Mental Equilibrium

Without a care for the result, do what you have to do with a balanced mind.
Success and failure are the same to the inspired worker.

बुद्धियुक्तो जहातीह उभे सुकृतदुष्कृते ।
तस्माद्योगाय युज्यस्व योगः कर्मसु कौशलम् ।।२-५०।।

*buddhiyukto jahātīha ubhe suktṛtaduṣkṛte,*
*tasmādyogāya yujyasva yogaḥ karmasu kauśalam. (2-50)*

Endowed with balance of mind, one detaches from the results of both good and bad actions. Therefore be in Yoga. Skill in action is Yoga.

## Skill in Action

A resolute intellect is not swayed
by anything – good or bad.
Dexterity in action comes when you are engrossed
in the action and not in yourself.

यदा संहरते चायं कूर्मोऽङ्गानीव सर्वशः ।
इन्द्रियाणीन्द्रियार्थेभ्यस्तस्य प्रज्ञा प्रतिष्ठिता ।।२-५८।।

*yadā saṁharate cāyaṁ kūrmo'ṅgānīva sarvaśaḥ,
indriyāṇīndriyārthebhyastasya prajñā pratiṣṭhitā. (2-58)*

Just as a tortoise withdraws its limbs, by withdrawing his sense organs from sense objects, a person's wisdom remains steady.

## Learn to say NO!

Wisdom is to say a firm "NO" to anything that threatens to snatch away your freedom. You can be happy without all of it. What you seek is already with you.

ध्यायतो विषयान्पुंसः सङ्गस्तेषूपजायते ।
सङ्गात्सञ्जायते कामः कामात्क्रोधोऽभिजायते ।।२-६२।।
क्रोधाद्भवति सम्मोहः सम्मोहात्स्मृतिविभ्रमः ।
स्मृतिभ्रंशाद् बुद्धिनाशो बुद्धिनाशात्प्रणश्यति ।।२-६३।।

*dhyāyato viṣayānpuṁsaḥ saṅgasteṣūpajāyate,*
*saṅgātsañjāyate kāmaḥ kāmātkrodho'bhijāyate.* (2-62)
*krodhādbhavati sammohaḥ sammohātsmṛtivibhramaḥ,*
*smṛtibhraṁśād buddhināśo buddhināśātpraṇaśyati.* (2-63)

Thinking about sense objects brings an attachment towards them. Attachment breeds desire and desire leads to frustration, which in turn leads to delusion. When you are deluded, you lose your memory and with the loss of memory, the power of discrimination is destroyed. In the absence of discrimination, the individual perishes.

## How you land yourself in HOT SOUP

1) You keep thinking about something.
2) You grow fond of it.
3) You want it badly.
4) If you do not get it, you get wild.
5) You are so wild that you cannot see who you are, what is around you, or what to do.
6) And still, you act!

Lo & behold! You have landed yourself squarely in HOT SOUP.

नियतं कुरु कर्म त्वं कर्म ज्यायो ह्यकर्मणः ।
शरीरयात्रापि च ते न प्रसिद्ध्येदकर्मणः ।।३-८।।

*niyataṁ kuru karma tvaṁ karma jyāyo hyakarmaṇaḥ,*
*śarīrayātrāpi ca te na prasiddhyedakarmaṇaḥ. (3-8)*

Perform your duty, for action is superior to inaction. Even the body cannot be maintained without action.

## Be Proactive

A rusty mind rots. So strive to revive the vigour to achieve bigger and better.

यज्ञार्थात्कर्मणोऽन्यत्र लोकोऽयं कर्मबन्धनः ।
तदर्थं कर्म कौन्तेय मुक्तसङ्गः समाचर ।।३-९।।

*yajñārthātkarmaṇo'nyatra loko'yaṁ karmabandhanaḥ,*
*tadarthaṁ karma kaunteya muktasaṅgaḥ samācara. (3-9)*

Except action performed for sacrifice, every kind of action done in this world is binding. Hence, Arjuna, perform action with the spirit of sacrifice alone, free from all attachment.

## Be The One

Feel – for all.
Work – for a great cause.
Give – the maximum.
Reach – the highest.
Be – The One.

यद्यदाचरति श्रेष्ठस्तत्तदेवेतरो जनः ।
स यत्प्रमाणं कुरुते लोकस्तदनुवर्तते ।।३-२१।।

*yadyadācarati śreṣṭhastattadevetaro janaḥ,*
*sa yatpramāṇaṁ kurute lokastadanuvartate. (3-21)*

Whatever a great man does, people follow. Whatever standard he sets, the world pursues.

**Leadership**

A true leader creates the mould from which other leaders emerge.
He will transform a face in the crowd into one the crowd faces.

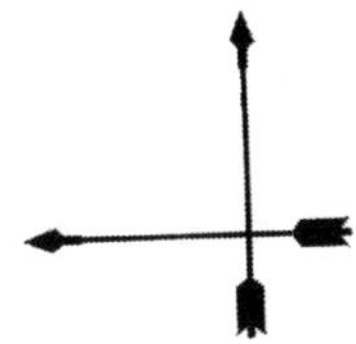

मयि सर्वाणि कर्माणि सन्न्यस्याध्यात्मचेतसा ।
निराशीर्निर्ममो भूत्वा युध्यस्व विगतज्वरः ।।३-३०।।

*mayi sarvāṇi karmāṇi sannyasyādhyātmacetasā,*
*nirāśirnirmamo bhūtvā yudhyasva vigatajvaraḥ. (3-30)*

With the mind centred on the Divine, devote all actions to the Higher. Free from hope, egotism and devoid of anxiety, face life.

## Be in the Present

Centred in the core of your personality, go all out. Free yourself from the dead past and the unborn future.
This moment is your only chance to create, advance and achieve.

इन्द्रियस्येन्द्रियस्यार्थे रागद्वेषौ व्यवस्थितौ ।
तयोर्न वशमागच्छेत्तौ ह्यस्य परिपन्थिनौ ।।३-३४।।

*indriyasyendriyasyārthe rāgadveṣau vyavasthitau,*
*tayorna vaśamāgacchettau hyasya paripanthinau.* (3-34)

The senses drive one to feel attraction or aversion towards worldly objects; do not be influenced by the senses, for they are our enemies.

## The Art of Right Contact

Stand at the gateway of your mind.
Choose your thoughts.
Master yourself.
This is the Art of Right Contact.

श्रेयान्स्वधर्मो विगुणः परधर्मात्स्वनुष्ठितात् ।
स्वधर्मे निधनं श्रेयः परधर्मो भयावहः ।।३-३५।।

*śreyānsvadharmo viguṇaḥ paradharmātsvanuṣṭhitāt,*
*svadharme nidhanaṁ śreyaḥ paradharmo bhayāvahaḥ.* (3-35)

Acting according to one's own nature, even though imperfectly, is better than doing the 'duties' of another efficiently. It is better to die engaged in duties that are in line with our nature, because performing the 'duty' of another is dangerous and detrimental.

## Follow Your Passion

Discover that which is inborn and natural in you.
Put it into selfless action.
Write your own unique story – do not copy.

यदा यदा हि धर्मस्य ग्लानिर्भवति भारत ।
अभ्युत्थानमधर्मस्य तदात्मानं सृजाम्यहम् ।।४-७।।

*yadā yadā hi dharmasya glānirbhavati bhārata,*
*abhyutthānamadharmasya tadātmānaṁ sṛjāmyaham.* (4-7)

Whenever there is a decay of righteousness and a rise of unrighteousness, O Bhārata, then the Divine manifests.

## Dare to Bring a Change

When troubles prevail, that is the right time to bring a positive change. So rise up, because the time is right.

ये यथा मां प्रपद्यन्ते तांस्तथैव भजाम्यहम् ।
मम वर्त्मानुवर्तन्ते मनुष्याः पार्थ सर्वशः ।।४-११।।

*ye yathā māṁ prapadyante tāṁstathaiva bhajāmyaham,*
*mama vartmānuvartante manuṣyāḥ pārtha sarvaśaḥ. (4-11)*

In whatever manner people worship Me, I reward them accordingly. In all the available paths, everyone follows My path alone, O Arjuna!

## The Power of Attraction

You have the power to attract anything in the universe. The resources are already with you. What will you do with them? The choice is yours.

चातुर्वर्ण्यं मया सृष्टं गुणकर्मविभागशः।
तस्य कर्तारमपि मां विद्ध्यकर्तारमव्ययम् ।।४-१३।।

*cāturvarṇyaṁ mayā sṛṣṭaṁ guṇakarmavibhāgaśaḥ,*
*tasya kartāramapi māṁ viddhyakartāramavyayam.* (4-13)

Based on one's qualities and actions, the four-fold castes have been created by the Divine. Though the caste distinction is by the Divine, know that the Divine itself is the non-doer and is unchanging.

## Re-Cast your Caste

Each of us belongs to one of these universal castes: Thinkers, Rulers, Money-makers and Labourers. Not birth, but mental qualities and actions decide the caste in which you are cast. Through cultivating noble qualities, you can re-cast your caste. The life principle in you and me (the cast-maker) is, however, cast(e)-free.

यदृच्छालाभसन्तुष्टो द्वन्द्वातीतो विमत्सरः।
समः सिद्धावसिद्धौ च कृत्वापि न निबध्यते ।।४-२२।।

*yadṛcchālābhasantuṣṭo dvandvātīto vimatsaraḥ,*
*samaḥ siddhāvasiddhau ca kṛtvāpi na nibadhyate. (4-22)*

Content with what comes to him without effort, free from the pairs of opposites and envy, even-minded in success and failure, though acting, the wise man is not attached.

## Act Fearlessly

Act fearlessly, ready to meet any consequence of your actions. This is the formula for complete and enduring success.

न हि ज्ञानेन सदृशं पवित्रमिह विद्यते ।
तत्स्वयं योगसंसिद्धः कालेनात्मनि विन्दति ।।४-३८।।

*na hi jñānena sadṛśaṁ pavitramiha vidyate,
tatsvayaṁ yogasaṁsiddhaḥ kālenātmani vindati.* (4-38)

There is nothing more purifying than transcendental Knowledge. One who is perfect in devotion realises this understanding within himself in due course.

## Experiencing Knowledge

Knowledge provides a clear vision. Sustain the vision, bring it into action and make it your mission. Thus achieve perfection.

श्रद्धावाँल्लभते ज्ञानं तत्परः संयतेन्द्रियः ।
ज्ञानं लब्ध्वा परां शान्तिमचिरेणाधिगच्छति ।।४-३९।।

*śraddhāvāṁllabhate jñānaṁ tatparaḥ saṁyatendriyaḥ,*
*jñānaṁ labdhvā parāṁ śāntimacireṇādhigacchati. (4-39)*

One who has faith, devotion to attaining Knowledge, and who has mastered the senses, will obtain Knowledge Absolute. With this Knowledge Absolute he quickly attains the supreme peace.

## Self-Mastery

Cultivate Conviction –
Stubbornly believe in your infinite potential.
Find your Focus –
Give your undivided attention to realising this potential.
Master your Mind –
From this comes courage of action.
Practice this and be incessantly happy.

अज्ञश्चाश्रद्दधानश्च संशयात्मा विनश्यति ।
नायं लोकोऽस्ति न परो न सुखं संशयात्मनः ।।४-४०।।

*ajñaścāśraddadhānaśca saṁśayātmā vinaśyati,*
*nāyaṁ loko'sti na paro na sukhaṁ saṁśayātmanaḥ.* (4-40)

Those who are ignorant, faithless and suspicious are lost. There is neither happiness nor success in any world for the doubting soul.

## Ignorance: Bliss or Blister?

Ignorance and suspicion sap the joy from life, because ignorance blinds the mind and doubt poisons it.

ब्रह्मण्याधाय कर्माणि सङ्गं त्यक्त्वा करोति यः ।
लिप्यते न स पापेन पद्मपत्रमिवाम्भसा ।।५-१०।।

*brahmaṇyādhāya karmāṇi saṅgaṁ tyaktvā karoti yaḥ,*
*lipyate na sa pāpena padmapatramivāmbhasā. (5-10)*

He who abandons attachment and dedicates actions to the Infinite is not tainted by wrong doing, just as a lotus leaf remains unaffected by the water on it.

## Real Fun

The wise man's answers to LIFE:
Where are you? HERE.
What time is it? NOW.
Who are you? THIS MOMEMT.

Thus he enjoys every experience and yet,
he is unaffected by any.

अनाश्रितः कर्मफलं कार्यं कर्म करोति यः ।
स सन्न्यासी च योगी च न निरग्निर्न चाक्रियः ।।६-१ ।।

*anāśritaḥ karmaphalaṁ kāryaṁ karma karoti yaḥ,*
*sa sannyāsī ca yogī ca na niragnirna cākriyaḥ. (6-1)*

The man who performs his duties without depending upon the results of his actions is a Realised Man and a Yogi, not a man who does no action and has no motivation.

## Face Life, Make Life

Face life, even when it turns its back on you. How? Do your work OUT OF JOY and NOT FOR JOY. With this attitude, fight. Do not take flight.

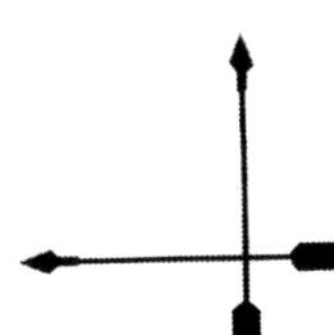

उद्धरेदात्मनात्मानं नात्मानमवसादयेत् ।
आत्मैव ह्यात्मनो बन्धुरात्मैव रिपुरात्मनः ।।६-५।।

*uddharedātmanātmānaṁ nātmānamavasādayet,*
*ātmaiva hyātmano bandhurātmaiva ripurātmanaḥ. (6-5)*

Let a man uplift himself by himself, and let him not drag himself down, for he alone is both the friend and the enemy of himself.

## Lift Yourself by Yourself

Lift yourself by yourself. Bridge the gap between who you are and who you want to be. Stand firm in your ideals, and conquer your limitations. The path to perfection is a ONE-WAY highway. Walk the path, or stay where you are. It is up to you.

यतो यतो निश्चरति मनश्चञ्चलमस्थिरम् ।
ततस्ततो नियम्यैतदात्मन्येव वशं नयेत् ।।६-२६।।

*yato yato niścarati manaścañcalamasthiram,*
*tatastato niyamyaitadātmanyeva vaśaṁ nayet. (6-26)*

When the turbulent mind wanders away from a cause, restrain it and bring it back under the control of the Self alone.

**Bounce Back**

Do not let the mind bounce away from the goal.
If it does, BOUNCE BACK!

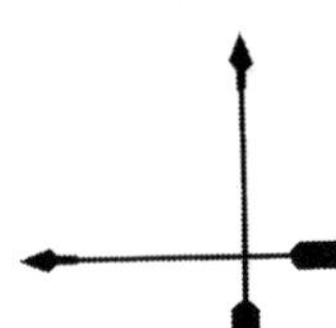

सर्वभूतस्थमात्मानं सर्वभूतानि चात्मनि ।
ईक्षते योगयुक्तात्मा सर्वत्र समदर्शनः ।।६-२९।।

*sarvabhūtasthamātmānaṁ sarvabhūtāni cātmani,*
*īkṣate yogayuktātmā sarvatra samadarśanaḥ. (6-29)*

He who is disciplined in yoga sees the Divinity existing in all beings and all beings existing in the Divine. He sees the equality everywhere.

## Tune In

When you are in tune with yourself, you are in tune with the universe. So you begin to see that all things in creation are expressions of the same love – just as all waves are expressions of the same water. Essentially, we are all ONE.

यो मां पश्यति सर्वत्र सर्वं च मयि पश्यति ।
तस्याहं न प्रणश्यामि स च मे न प्रणश्यति ।।६-३०।।

*yo māṁ paśyati sarvatra sarvaṁ ca mayi paśyati,*
*tasyāhaṁ na praṇaśyāmi sa ca me na praṇaśyati. (6-30)*

He who sees Me everywhere and sees everything in Me, he never gets separated from Me nor do I get separated from him.

## The Vision of Oneness

Once you learn to see the maker in all things made, and all things made as the maker himself, then you and the maker are one and the same.

असंयतात्मना योगो दुष्प्राप इति मे मतिः।
वश्यात्मना तु यतता शक्योऽवाप्तुमुपायतः।।६-३६।।

*asaṁyatāmanā yogo duṣprāpa iti me matiḥ,*
*vaśyātmanā tu yatatā śakyo'vāptumupāyataḥ. (6-36)*

Yoga, I think, is hard to be attained by one who is uncontrolled; but the self-controlled individual, striving, can obtain it by proper means.

## Entertain only the Essential

Preserve your energy. Use it only for your goal. If you dissipate your energy in idle activities, the goal will always remain out of reach.

मत्तः परतरं नान्यत्किञ्चिदस्ति धनञ्जय ।
मयि सर्वमिदं प्रोतं सूत्रे मणिगणा इव ।।७-७।।

*mattaḥ parataraṁ nānyatkiñcidasti dhanañjaya,*
*mayi sarvamidaṁ protaṁ sūtre maṇigaṇā iva. (7-7)*

O Winner of wealth! There is nothing higher than the Divine. Everything rests on Me like pearls strung on a thread.

## Holistic Perception

The fractional perceiver sees only individual beads. The holistic perceiver sees the thread that HOLDS the beads together in a beautiful garland. Holistic perception leads to ultimate perfection.

बलं बलवतां चाहं कामरागविवर्जितम् ।
धर्माविरुद्धो भूतेषु कामोऽस्मि भरतर्षभ ।।७-११।।

*balaṁ balavatāṁ cāhaṁ kāmarāgavivarjitam,*
*dharmāviruddho bhūteṣu kāmo'smi bharatarṣabha. (7-11)*

I am the strength of the strong – devoid of desire and attachment. In all beings, I am the righteous desire, O best among the Bharatas.

## Right is Might

Set your sights high. Walk with burning aspiration on the path of righteousness. Thus achieve the best and share with the rest.

दैवी ह्येषा गुणमयी मम माया दुरत्यया ।
मामेव ये प्रपद्यन्ते मायामेतां तरन्ति ते ।।७-१४।।

*daivī hyeṣā guṇamayī mama māyā duratyayā,*
*māmeva ye prapadyante māyāmetāṁ taranti te. (7-14)*

My divine illusion consists of qualities that are difficult to cross over. Those who devote themselves to Me alone shall cross over this illusion.

## Go Beyond

You experience limitations because the mind is limited. To drop your limitations, anchor yourself to the Absolute which is beyond the mind.

चतुर्विधा भजन्ते मां जनाः सुकृतिनोऽर्जुन ।
आर्तो जिज्ञासुरर्थार्थी ज्ञानी च भरतर्षभ ।।७-१६।।

तेषां ज्ञानी नित्ययुक्त एकभक्तिर्विशिष्यते ।
प्रियो हि ज्ञानिनोऽत्यर्थमहं स च मम प्रियः ।।७-१७।।

*caturvidhā bhajante māṁ janāḥ sukṛtino'rjuna,*
*ārto jijñsurarthārthī jñānī ca bharatarṣabha. (7-16)*

*teṣāṁ jñānī nityayukta ekabhaktirviśiṣyate,*
*priyo hi jñānino'tyarthamahaṁ sa ca mama priyaḥ. (7-17)*

O Arjuna, among the pious, four kinds of men worship Me: the distressed, those who desire wealth, the inquisitive and those seeking knowledge of the Truth Absolute.

Of these, the man seeking Knowledge and who is engaged in pure devotional service is the best. He who is fond of Me is dear to Me.

## The Four Kinds of Seekers

There are 4 types of seekers in this world:

1. Those who just want to feel better.
2. Those who just want to know better.
3. Those who just want to have better.
4. Those who want the best – eternal freedom.

Of these, the fourth is the wisest and most easily rewarded.

यो यो यां यां तनुं भक्तः श्रद्धयार्चितुमिच्छति ।
तस्य तस्याचलां श्रद्धां तामेव विदधाम्यहम् ।।७-२१।।

*yo yo yāṁ yāṁ tanuṁ bhaktaḥ śraddhayārcitumicchati,*
*tasya tasyācalāṁ śraddhāṁ tāmeva vidadhāmyaham. (7-21)*

O Bhāratīya, success is directly proportional to the depth of faith we have, both in ourselves and in the goal. I make this faith firm and steady.

## The Logic of Destiny

What you regularly encourage and consistently cultivate becomes your faith and your destiny.

यं यं वापि स्मरन्भावं त्यजत्यन्ते कलेवरम् ।
तं तमेवैति कौन्तेय सदा तद्भावभावितः ।।८-६।।

*yaṁ yaṁ vāpi smaranbhāvaṁ tyajatyante kalevaram,*
*taṁ tamevaiti kaunteya sadā tadbhāvabhāvitaḥ. (8-6)*

Whenever one leaves the body thinking of any being to that being alone he goes. This is because of his constant thought of that being.

## Thoughts become Things

Whatever are your deepest thoughts, towards that you will go. Even death cannot stop this journey.

अनन्यचेताः सततं यो मां स्मरति नित्यशः ।
तस्याहं सुलभः पार्थ नित्ययुक्तस्य योगिनः ।।८-१४।।

*ananyacetāḥ satataṁ yo māṁ smarati nityaśaḥ,*
*tasyāhaṁ sulabhaḥ pārtha nityayuktasya yoginaḥ. (8-14)*

O Arjuna! One who is focused on the Higher, day in and day out, is sure to reach the Higher realms .

## Focus on the Bull's Eye

Remember your target always – think of it day in and day out. Leave no room for other thoughts and you will attain it effortlessly.

अनन्याश्चिन्तयन्तो मां ये जनाः पर्युपासते ।
तेषां नित्याभियुक्तानां योगक्षेमं वहाम्यहम् ।।९-२२।।

*ananyāścintayanto māṁ ye janāḥ paryupāsate,*
*teṣaṁ nityābhiyuktānāṁ yogakṣemaṁ vahāmyaham.* (9-22)

Those who single pointedly seek Me with self-control, I secure what they seek (yoga) and preserve what they have (kṣema).

## The Secret of Success

Fix your goal, focus your energy, fight all distractions. Thus secure your present and your future.

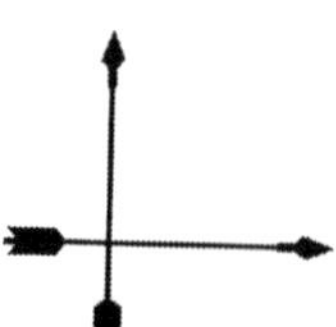

यत्करोषि यदश्नासि यज्जुहोषि ददासि यत् ।
यत्तपस्यसि कौन्तेय तत्कुरुष्व मदर्पणम् ।।९-२७।।

*yatkaroṣi yadaśnāsi yajjuhoṣi dadāsi yat,*
*yattapasyasi kaunteya tatkuruṣva madarpaṇam.* (9-27)

Whatever you do, whatever you eat, whatever you offer in sacrifice, whatever you give in charity, whatever you practise as austerity, O Kaunteya, do it as an offering to Me.

## Mindfulness

Be mindful in even the minutest of matters.
That is what matters most.

अपि चेत्सुदुराचारो भजते मामनन्यभाक् ।
साधुरेव स मन्तव्यः सम्यग्व्यवसितो हि सः ।।९-३०।।

*api cetsudurācāro bhajate māmananyabhāk,*
*sādhureva sa mantavyaḥ samyagvyavasito hi saḥ. (9-30)*

Even if a person of very heinous behaviour is engaged in devotional service to Me, he is considered saintly as he is on the righteous path.

## Change your Thoughts, Change your Destiny

Disconnect from your guilty past.
TAKE OUT the trash from your mind and TAKE UP a firm resolve. Apply yourself to it constantly.
Sinners become saints when thoughts change.
So discover the saint in you!

क्षिप्रं भवति धर्मात्मा शश्वच्छान्तिं निगच्छति ।
कौन्तेय प्रतिजानीहि न मे भक्तः प्रणश्यति ।।९-३१।।

*kṣipraṁ bhavati dharmātmā śaśvacchāntiṁ nigacchati,*
*kaunteya pratijānīhi na me bhaktaḥ praṇaśyati. (9-31)*

As soon as he becomes righteous and attains eternal peace, O Kaunteya, know for certain that My devotee will never perish.

## Just Do it!

There is nothing more satisfying than walking courageously on the right path your heart has resolved to take. So do not think twice. Walk sincerely towards your noble goal. Only victory will be yours.

मच्चित्ता मद्गतप्राणा बोधयन्तः परस्परम् ।
कथयन्तश्च मां नित्यं तुष्यन्ति च रमन्ति च ।।१०-९।।

*maccittā madgataprāṇā bodhayantaḥ parasparam,*
*kathayantaśca māṁ nityaṁ tuṣyanti ca ramanti ca. (10-9)*

With their minds solely focused on the Divine, with their senses absorbed in the Divine, enlightening one another, and ever speaking of the Divine, they are satisfied and delighted.

## Positive Peers

Surround yourself with those who bring out the best in you, who remind you of the greater things in life. In their company, think only the purest thoughts, say only the purest words, do only the purest deeds and you will be forever delighted.

तेषां सततयुक्तानां भजतां प्रीतिपूर्वकम् ।
ददामि बुद्धियोगं तं येन मामुपयान्ति ते ।।१०-१०।।

*teṣāṁ satatayuktānāṁ bhajatāṁ prītipūrvakam,*
*dadāmi buddhiyogaṁ taṁ yena māmupayānti te. (10-10)*

To those who are ever steadfast, worshipping Me with love, I give buddhi-yoga (the stability of knowledge), by which they come to Me.

## Recipe for Excellence

1) Steadfastness in the pursuit of a higher goal.
2) Love for both the goal as well as the means to attain it.

तस्मात्त्वमुत्तिष्ठ यशो लभस्व
जित्वा शत्रून्भुङ्क्ष्व राज्यं समृद्धम् ।
मयैवैते निहताः पूर्वमेव
निमित्तमात्रं भव सव्यसाचिन् ।।११-३३।।

*tasmāttvamuttiṣṭha yaśo labhasva*
*jitvā śatrūnbhuṅkṣva rājyaṁ samṛddham,*
*mayaivaite nihatāḥ pūrvameva*
*nimittamātraṁ bhava savyasācin. (11-33)*

Therefore arise and win glory. Conquer your enemies and take pleasure in sovereignty. Your enemies have already been slain by Me. You are just an instrument in the battle.

## Instrument of Inspiration

Surrender. Be an instrument in the unseen hands of the universe. Say a bold 'YES' to the cosmic intelligence. Stand up and enjoy the success that it showers upon you

भक्त्या त्वनन्यया शक्य अहमेवंविधोऽर्जुन ।
ज्ञातुं द्रष्टुं च तत्त्वेन प्रवेष्टुं च परन्तप ।।११-५४।।

*bhaktyā tvananyayā śakya ahamevaṁvidho'rjuna,*
*jñātuṁ draṣṭuṁ ca tattvena praveṣṭuṁ ca parantapa. (11-54)*

Only by single-minded devotion can I be known, seen and entered into, O destroyer of enemies!

## Devotion

Love your goal.
Give yourself up to your goal.
Become one with your goal.
That is devotion.

यस्मान्नोद्विजते लोको लोकान्नोद्विजते च यः ।
हर्षामर्षभयोद्वेगैर्मुक्तो यः स च मे प्रियः ।।१२-१५।।

*yasmānnodvijate loko lokānnodvijate ca yaḥ,*
*harṣāmarṣabhayodvegairmukto yaḥ sa ca me priyaḥ.* (12-15)

He who perturbs no one and who never gets disturbed by anyone, who is not overcome by happiness, impatience, fear and anxiety, is dear to Me.

## Man of Perfection

He who gives no sorrow nor accepts any, who has equipoise in all situations, who has conquered his mind – He is a man of perfection.

समः शत्रौ च मित्रे च तथा मानापमानयोः।
शीतोष्णसुखदुःखेषु समः सङ्गविवर्जितः ।।१२-१८।।

*samaḥ śatrau ca mitre ca tathā mānāpamānayoḥ,*
*śītoṣṇasukhaduḥkeṣu samaḥ saṅgavivarjitaḥ. (12-18)*

A person who is even-minded and who sees friends and enemies, honour and disgrace, heat and cold, happiness and anger, blame and praise, all in the same light, is free from attachment.

## Balance of Mind

He who is unconditional in all relationships, who is not carried away by fame or shame, who can withstand all physical conditions – He is truly free from attachment.

तुल्यनिन्दास्तुतिर्मौनी सन्तुष्टो येन केनचित् ।
अनिकेतः स्थिरमतिर्भक्तिमान्मे प्रियो नरः ।।१२-१९।।

*tulyanindāstutirmaunī santuṣṭo yena kenacit,*
*aniketaḥ sthiramatirbhaktimānme priyo naraḥ. (12-19)*

A composed person (always content) has got clarity in thoughts and is always engaged in achieving the higher cause. Such a person is dear to me.

## Evolve, Don't Revolve

Qualities of an Evolved Man

1) He is always composed.
2) He is a man of few words.
3) He is content with anything.
4) He constantly pushes his comfort zone.
5) He is full of love.

असक्तिरनभिष्वङ्गः पुत्रदारगृहादिषु ।
नित्यं च समचित्तत्वमिष्टानिष्टोपपत्तिषु ।।१३-१०।।

*asaktiranabhiṣvaṅgaḥ putradāragṛhādiṣu,*
*nityaṁ ca samacittatvamiṣṭāniṣṭopapattiṣu. (13-10)*

Detachment and not identifying oneself with all relations makes for a balanced mind in both the desirable and the undesirable situations of life.

## Free your Mind

When the mind sticks to things, it gets sick. A dependent mind is pathetic, while an independent mind is energetic. Free your mind – Tap into your energy source.

अविभक्तं च भूतेषु विभक्तमिव च स्थितम् ।
भूतभर्तृ च तज्ज्ञेयं ग्रसिष्णु प्रभविष्णु च ।।१३-१७।।

*avibhaktaṁ ca bhūteṣu vibhaktamiva ca sthitam,*
*bhūtabhartṛ ca tajjñeyaṁ grasiṣṇu prabhaviṣṇu ca. (13-17)*

He is undivided, though He exists as if divided in beings. He is to be known as the supporter of the beings. He generates and He devours.

ॐ

**3 in 1**

The all-pervading indivisible Truth creates, sustains and destroys the world. It is the changeless base in and through all the change in the world.

सत्त्वं सुखे सञ्जयति रजः कर्मणि भारत ।
ज्ञानमावृत्य तु तमः प्रमादे सञ्जयत्युत ।।१४-९।।

*sattvaṁ sukhe sañjayati rajaḥ karmaṇi bhārata,*
*jñānamāvṛtya tu tamaḥ pramāde sañjayatyuta.* (14-9)

Sattva brings happiness, Rajas attaches to action and Tamas leads to laziness/carelessness.

## Minding the Mind

There are three temperaments of the mind - Clarity, Passion and Delusion.

Clarity brings happiness.

Passion brings action.

Delusion brings confusion.

Which is predominant in you ?

गुणानेतानतीत्य त्रीन्देही देहसमुद्भवान् ।
जन्ममृत्युजरादुःखैर्विमुक्तोऽमृतमश्नुते ।।१४-२०।।

*guṇānetānatītya trīndehī dehasamudbhavān,*
*janmamṛtyujarāduḥkhairvimukto'mṛtamaśnute.* (14-20)

Immortality is attained by the one who has crossed the three guṇas out of which the body is evolved. He is free from birth, death, pain and decay.

**Cross Over**

Attain the Infinite and then nothing can hold you back. NOTHING.

निर्मानमोहा जितसङ्गदोषा अध्यात्मनित्या विनिवृत्तकामाः ।
द्वन्द्वैर्विमुक्ताः सुखदुःखसञ्ज्ञैर्गच्छन्त्यमूढाः पदमव्ययं तत् ।।१५-५।।

*nirmānamohā jitasaṅgadoṣā-*
*adhyātmanityā vinivṛttakāmāḥ,*
*dvandvairvimuktāḥ sukhaduḥkhasaṅjñair-*
*gacchantyamūḍhāḥ padamavyayaṁ tat. (15-5)*

Those who are free from pride, delusion and false attachment, those who dwell in the eternal, who have turned away from material desires and are free from the dualities of joy and sorrow - they attain that eternal goal.

## Qualities of a Champion

What sort of person reaches his goal?
One who is driven but not desire-ridden.
One who is ambitious but not attached.
One who is persevering but not proud.
One who is grounded but not greedy.
One who is stable but not superficial.

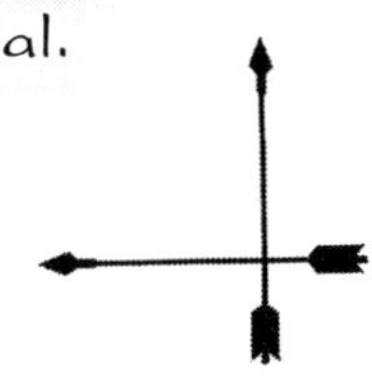

यदादित्यगतं तेजो जगद्भासयतेऽखिलम् ।
यच्चन्द्रमसि यच्चाग्नौ तत्तेजो विद्धि मामकम् ।।१५-१२।।

*yadādityagataṁ tejo jagadbhāsayate'khilam,*
*yaccandramasi yaccāgnau tattejo viddhi māmakam. (15-12)*

The radiance of the sun, the moon and the fire that illuminates the world, all stem from Me.

## Light up your Life

The light in the sun, moon and fire is the same light which is within you. That light is pure Consciousness – the life-giving force of the universe.

अहं वैश्वानरो भूत्वा प्राणिनां देहमाश्रितः ।
प्राणापानसमायुक्तः पचाम्यन्नं चतुर्विधम् ।।१५-१४।।

*ahaṁ vaisvānaro bhūtvā prāṇināṁ dehamāśritaḥ,*
*prāṇāpānasamāyuktaḥ pacāmyannaṁ caturvidham. (15-14)*

I become the fire of digestion residing in the bodies of all living beings. Then, in accordance with the incoming and outgoing life air, I digest the four kinds of food.

## The Spark that Sustains

How does a breath of air become the breath of life? How does the breath of life become the pulse of life? How does the pulse of life become the warmth of life?

Enquire into the nature of that spark of life.

अभयं सत्त्वसंशुद्धिर्ज्ञानयोगव्यवस्थितिः ।
दानं दमश्च यज्ञश्च स्वाध्यायस्तप आर्जवम् ।।१६-१।।

*abhayaṁ satvasaṁśuddhirjñānayogavyavasthitiḥ,*
*dānaṁ damaśca yajñaśca svādhyāyastapa ārjavam. (16-1)*

The supreme Being said: fearlessness, purity of heart, loyalty in spiritual knowledge, charity, sense control, sacrifice, study of the Vedas, austerity, virtue . . .

## Qualities of a Dynamic Leader

1) Fearlessness
2) Purity of heart
3) Steadfastness in knowledge
4) Generosity
5) Discipline
6) Sacrifice
7) Study and Reading
8) Straightforwardness . . .

अहिंसा सत्यमक्रोधस्त्यागः शान्तिरपैशुनम् ।
दया भूतेष्वलोलुप्त्वं मार्दवं ह्रीरचापलम् ।।१६-२।।

*ahiṁsā satyamakrodhastyāgaḥ śāntirapaiśunam,*
*dayā bhūteṣvaloluptvaṁ mārdavaṁ hrīracāpalam. (16-2)*

Non-violence, truthfulness, absence of anger, renunciation, tranquility, aversion to criticising others, compassion, freedom from greed, gentleness, modesty, determination...

## Qualities of a Dynamic Leader

9) Harmlessness
10) Truthfulness
11) Patience
12) Renunciation
13) Peacefulness
14) Honesty
15) Compassion
16) Moderation
17) Gentleness
18) Modesty
19) Stability

तेजः क्षमा धृतिः शौचमद्रोहो नातिमानिता ।
भवन्ति सम्पदं दैवीमभिजातस्य भारत ।।१६-३।।

*tejaḥ kṣamā dhṛtiḥ śaucamadroho nātimānitā,*
*bhavanti sampadaṁ daivīmabhijātasya bhārata. (16-3)*

Courage, forgiveness, fortitude, purity and freedom from hatred, absence of pride. Those who are endowed with these are of divine nature.

## Qualities of a Dynamic Leader

20) Courage
21) Forgiveness
22) Fortitude
23) Purity
24) Freedom from hatred
25) Absence of pride.

Attain the above.
Be a dynamic leader like Kṛṣṇa.

दम्भो दर्पोऽभिमानश्च क्रोधः पारुष्यमेव च ।
अज्ञानं चाभिजातस्य पार्थ सम्पदमासुरीम् ।।१६-४।।

*dambho darpo'bhimānaśca krodhaḥ pāruṣyameva ca,*
*ajñānaṁ cābhijātasya pārtha sampadamāsurīm. (16-4)*

Firm on the above grounds, one's character is influenced neither by arrogance nor hypocrisy. Knowledge makes him aware that anger and fear are for the ignorant!

**What will bring a man's downfall?**

1) Hypocrisy
2) Arrogance
3) Self-conceit
4) Anger
5) Harshness
6) Ignorance

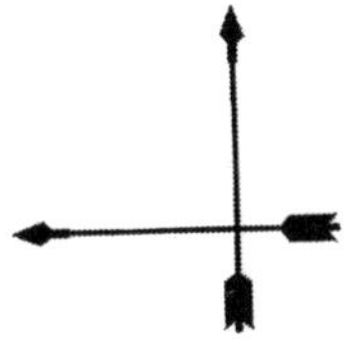

यः शास्त्रविधिमुत्सृज्य वर्तते कामकारतः ।
न स सिद्धिमवाप्नोति न सुखं न परां गतिम् ।।१६-२३।।

*yaḥ śāstravidhimutsṛjya vartate kāmakārataḥ,*
*na sa siddhimavāpnoti na sukhaṁ na parāṁ gatim. (16-23)*

One who discards scriptural injunctions and acts out of impulse attains neither perfection, happiness nor the ultimate goal of life.

## Complete the Incomplete

Does your life feel incomplete?
Have you been living recklessly?
You probably have not gone through the
'Manual of Life'.
The knowledge in it can transform you!

तस्माच्छास्त्रं प्रमाणं ते कार्याकार्यव्यवस्थितौ ।
ज्ञात्वा शास्त्रविधानोक्तं कर्म कर्तुमिहार्हसि ।।१६-२४।।

*tasmācchāstraṁ pramāṇaṁ te kāryākāryavyavasthitau,*
*jñātvā śāstravidhānoktaṁ karma kartumihārhasi. (16-24)*

Every appliance in this world comes with a manual. Unfortunately, our body does not come with one. Our rich heritage and culture have given us various texts which, if understood rightly, will guide us humans to live a humane life, to remove ignorance, to come out of our comfort zone, to eradicate our fears to break our shell!

## The 'Manual of Life'

Take the scriptures as your 'Manual of Life'. With them as your guiding light, take steps to succeed in the Goal of Life.

सत्त्वानुरूपा सर्वस्य श्रद्धा भवति भारत ।
श्रद्धामयोऽयं पुरुषो यो यच्छ्रद्धः स एव सः ।।१७-३।।

*sattvānurūpā sarvasya śraddhā bhavati bhārata,*
*śraddhāmayo'yaṁ puruṣo yo yacchraddhaḥ sa eva saḥ.* (17-3)

O Bhārata, know what you strongly believe in. As the faith, so the man. Faith lies in the secret energy of conviction to reach a definite chosen goal.

## You are your Convictions

Pick and choose your beliefs. Develop them into strong convictions.
Live according to them, stand for them and you will be undefeatable.

अनुद्वेगकरं वाक्यं सत्यं प्रियहितं च यत् ।
स्वाध्यायाभ्यसनं चैव वाङ्मयं तप उच्यते ।।१७-१५।।

*anudvegakaraṁ vākyaṁ satyaṁ priyahitaṁ ca yat,*
*svādhyāyābhyasanaṁ caive vāṅmayaṁ tapa ucyate. (17-15)*

Speech that causes no agitation, is truthful, pleasant, beneficial and is influenced by the practice and study of the Vedas constitutes austerity of speech.

**Optimal speech is:**

1) Well chosen
2) Truthful
3) Pleasant
4) Beneficial
5) Well informed

मनःप्रसादः सौम्यत्वं मौनमात्मविनिग्रहः ।
भावसंशुद्धिरित्येतत्तपो मानसमुच्यते ।।१७-१६।।

*manaḥprasādaḥ saumyatvaṁ maunamātmavinigrahaḥ,*
*bhāvasaṁśuddhirityetattapo mānasamucyate. (17-16)*

Serenity of mind, good-heartedness, silence, self-control, purity of nature - these together are called mental austerity.

## Mind Management

Mind becomes mighty when it is serene, silent, pure and well managed. Decrease the quantity of your thoughts and increase the quality of your thoughts.

यज्ञदानतपःकर्म न त्याज्यं कार्यमेव तत् ।
यज्ञो दानं तपश्चैव पावनानि मनीषिणाम् ।।१८-५।।

*yajñadānatapaḥkarma na tyājyaṁ kāryameva tat,*
*yajño dānaṁ tapaścaiva pāvanāni manīṣiṇām. (18-5)*

Perform charity, sacrifice and austerity. There are no exceptions or exemptions. They purify even the purest.

## Better than the Best

Unfold the beautiful depths of your personality:

1) Sacrifice – your weaknesses
2) Worship – the Ideal
3) Give – to charity
4) Master – the body and mind

चेतसा सर्वकर्माणि मयि सन्न्यस्य मत्परः ।
बुद्धियोगमुपाश्रित्य मच्चित्तः सततं भव ।।१८-५७।।

*cetasā sarvakarmāṇi mayi sannyasya matparaḥ,*
*buddhiyogamupāśritya maccittaḥ satataṁ bhava.* (18-57)

Surrender all actions unto Me. Use your power of discrimination and take Me as your highest goal. Keep your mind fixed upon Me.

**Lose Yourself**

Think only about divinity (Goal of life).
Act solely for divinity.
Surrender completely to the divine.
Divinity – Our Highest Goal.

मच्चित्तः सर्वदुर्गाणि मत्प्रसादात्तरिष्यसि ।
अथ चेत्त्वमहङ्कारान्न श्रोष्यसि विनङ्क्ष्यसि ।।१८-५८।।

*maccittaḥ sarvadurgāṇi matprasādāttariṣyasi,*
*atha cettvamahaṅkārānna śroṣyasi vinaṅkṣyasi. (18-58)*

If you fix your thoughts on the Supreme, you will conquer all your problems but if you act through egotism, thinking you know better, you will be doomed.

## Eradicate the Ego

An elevated mind persecutes all obstacles in its way. An egoistic mind persecutes itself. Give up your ego and fly high.

श्रद्धावाननसूयश्च शृणुयादपि यो नरः ।
सोऽपि मुक्तः शुभाँल्लोकान्प्राप्नुयात्पुण्यकर्मणाम् ।।१८-७१।।

*śraddhāvānanasūyaśca śṛṇuyādapi yo naraḥ,*
*so'pi muktaḥ śubhāṁllokānprāpnuyātpuṇyakarmaṇām.* (18-71)

One who listens to this full of faith and free from malice will become liberated and attain the auspicious worlds of the virtuous.

**Hear, Here!**

Entry to the wise words of the scriptures can be gained by cultivating a listening ear, an openness of mind, a readiness to learn and grow and the purest of intentions.

नष्टो मोहः स्मृतिर्लब्धा त्वत्प्रसादान्मयाच्युत ।
स्थितोऽस्मि गतसन्देहः करिष्ये वचनं तव ।।१८-७३।।

*naṣṭo mohaḥ smṛtirlabdhā tvatprasādānmayācyuta,*
*sthito'smi gatasandehaḥ kariṣye vacanaṁ tava. (18-73)*

Arjuna said: My delusion is destroyed, as I have now gained knowledge through your (Kṛṣṇa's) grace. I am firm, my doubts are gone. I will do according to your bidding.

**Meet your Mentor**

Find the right mentor. Align yourself with him. Awaken yourself. Then, awaken others. This is the best thing you can do with your life.

यत्र योगेश्वरः कृष्णो यत्र पार्थो धनुर्धरः ।
तत्र श्रीर्विजयो भूतिर्ध्रुवा नीतिर्मतिर्मम ।।१८-७८।।

*yatra yogeśvaraḥ kṛṣṇo yatra pārtho dhanurdharaḥ,*
*tatra śrīrvijayo bhūtirdhruvā nītirmatirmama. (18-78)*

Sañjaya said:

Wherever Kṛṣṇa, the Divine charioteer and Arjuna the archer are present, there will always be good fortune, victory, wealth, well-being and righteousness. This is my conviction.

## The Perfect Blend
## Knowledge + Action = Transformation

When the clarity of knowledge dawns upon you who possesses the readiness to act, you pick up your bow and arrow the way Arjuna did, ready to fight in the battlefield of life. Pour forth your talents and abilities to meet the need of the hour. Your potential to perform is at its peak.

Uttiṣṭha Bhārata!

Arise, O Son of this Great Land!

It's now time to apply these 70 precious gems of the Gītā in all fields of life.

Read, reflect, and re-live.

Go through Gītā. Grow through Gītā.

## Chinmaya yuva kendra (CHYK)

Chinmaya Yuva Kendra, or Chyk, is the global youth (14-28 yrs) wing of Chinmaya Mission. It aims to help youngsters discover their infinite strength and use it to serve society. Chyk activities include weekly discussion forums, workshops, leadership training, national camps and youth conventions, theatre, outdoor experiential learning, and publications.

Mission Statement: To empower youth with the vision, values, and dynamism for success in all fields.
Motto: Harnessing Youth Potential through Dynamic Spirituality

## Youth Empowerment Programme (YEP)

YEP is a one-year, work-study, residential value-based leadership programme for young college graduates who have a keen desire to learn Indian culture and serve India. With the motto of "Learn, Serve, and Grow", YEP empowers its participants, known as 'Yuva Veers,' through Vedantika studies, adventure, training in a variety of fieldwork, and hands-on internship, all of which are designed to promote individual inner strength and holistic transformation for a balanced lifestyle of personal growth and selfless service. Today more than 300 Yuva Veers across 7 different countries, are reaching out to more than 4 lakh youth and 3 lakh children through workshops, camps, college talks, etc.